# HOW TO IMPROVE AT <u>BASKETBALL</u>

### All the information you need to know to get on top of your game!

More than just instructional guides, the **HOW TO IMPROVE AT...** series gives you everything you need to achieve your goals—tips on technique, step-by-step demonstrations, nutritional advice, and the secrets of successful pro athletes. Excellent visual instructions and expert advice combine to act as your own personal trainer. These books aim to give you the know-how and confidence to improve your performance.

Studies have shown that an active approach to life makes you feel happier and less stressed. The easiest way to start is by taking up a new sport or improving your skills in an existing one. You simply have to choose an activity that enthuses you.

**HOW TO IMPROVE AT BASKETBALL** does not promise instant success. It simply gives you the tools to become the best at whatever you choose to do.

Every care has been taken to ensure that these instructions are safe to follow, but in the event of injury Crabtree Publishing shall not be liable for any injuries or damages.

## By Jim Drewett

## Crabtree Publishing Company
### www.crabtreebooks.com

**Cover:** San Antonio Spurs' basketball star Tim Duncan
**Special thank you to:** London Towers Basketball Club, Philip Gray and Elizabeth Wiggans
**Photography:** Roddy Paine Photographic Studios
**Illustrations:** John Alston, Robert MacGregor

**Photo credits:** Icon SMI/Kevin Reece: front cover; London Towers: p. 40 center and bottom, p. 41 top, center and bottom, p. 43 top and bottom; Empics: p. 43 middle; © Shutterstock.com: Morgan Lane Photography: p. 6 left; Aitor Bouzo Ateca: p. 27 bottom.

Library and Archives Canada Cataloguing in Publication

Drewett, Jim
    How to improve at basketball / Jim Drewett.

(How to improve at...)
Includes index.
ISBN 978-0-7787-3566-3 (bound).--ISBN 978-0-7787-3588-5 (pbk.)

    1. Basketball--Training--Juvenile literature. I. Title. II. Series.

GV885.1.D74 2007    j796.323    C2007-904705-X

Library of Congress Cataloging-in-Publication Data

Drewett, Jim.
  How to improve at basketball / Jim Drewett.
    p. cm. -- (How to improve at--)
  Includes index.
  ISBN-13: 978-0-7787-3566-3 (rlb)
  ISBN-10: 0-7787-3566-4 (rlb)
  ISBN-13: 978-0-7787-3588-5 (pb)
  ISBN-10: 0-7787-3588-5 (pb)
  1. Basketball for children--Training--Juvenile literature. I. Title. II. Series.

  GV885.35.D74 2008
  796.323'2--dc22    2007030187

## Crabtree Publishing Company
www.crabtreebooks.com    1-800-387-7650

**Published in Canada**
**Crabtree Publishing**
616 Welland Ave.
St. Catharines, Ontario
L2M 5V6

**Published in the United States**
**Crabtree Publishing**
PMB16A
350 Fifth Ave., Suite 3308
New York, NY 10118

**Published by CRABTREE PUBLISHING COMPANY**
Copyright © **2008**

# CONTENTS

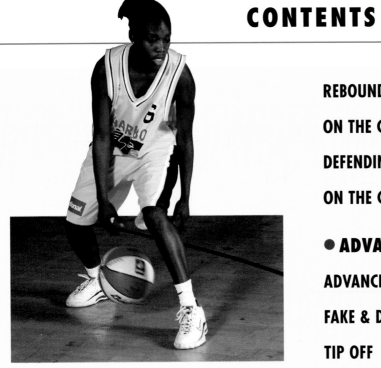

# INTRODUCTION

*Lightning quick and loaded with skill, basketball is one of the world's most popular games. Its flashiness and million-dollar superstars make it a fantastic spectator sport. Millions of people tune in every week to watch the NBA, or National Basketball Association. Basketball is also a great game to play, and we want this book to inspire you to get out there and shoot some hoops!*

## GUIDE TO SYMBOLS & ARROWS

*Throughout this book, you will find helpful illustrations to show you how to do a drill. Unless specified, these dots, lines, and arrows represent the following:*

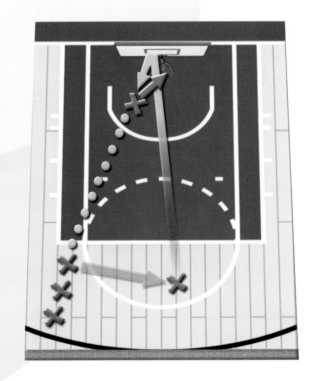

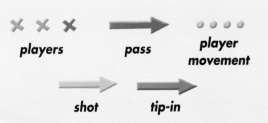

players     pass     player movement

shot     tip-in

# THE COURT

*B*asketball is not only popular, it is also one of the simplest sports to learn. The court shown here is for a proper game, but all you really need for a great game of basketball is a ball, a basket and a smooth floor.

## THE COURT

A pro basketball court is 94 feet (28.5 m) long and 50 feet (15 m) wide. The best courts have polished wooden flooring, although any smooth surface will do.

## THE BASKET & BACKBOARD

At each end of the court is a basket, which overhangs the baseline. The hoop is set 10 feet (3.05 m) from the ground. Behind the hoop is a backboard that is 6 feet x 3.5 feet (1.8 x 1.05 m). The ball can rebound off of this board and into the basket. On pro courts, the backboard is usually see-through, so it doesn't block the view of spectators.

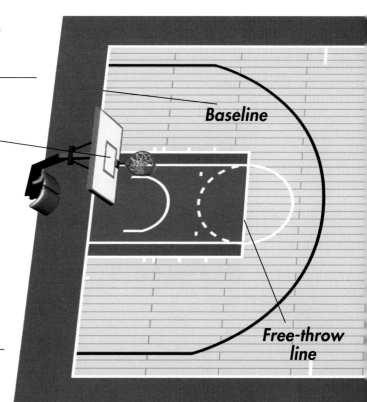

*Baseline*

*Free-throw line*

## TEAMS

Basketball teams usually have around ten to twelve players, but only five are allowed on the court at once. The coach decides which five players he or she wants on the court, and he or she can bring players on and off all through the game.

To move the ball, players can pass to a teammate, or they can dribble. Dribbling means bouncing the ball along the ground while walking or running.

The object of basketball is to score more points than the opposition. To score points, teams must score baskets – in other words, shoot the ball through their opponent's hoop. The amount of points given for a basket depends on where the player is standing when the ball is shot.

Players are only allowed to step inside their opponents' "key" for three seconds at a time (the areas colored blue in this diagram).

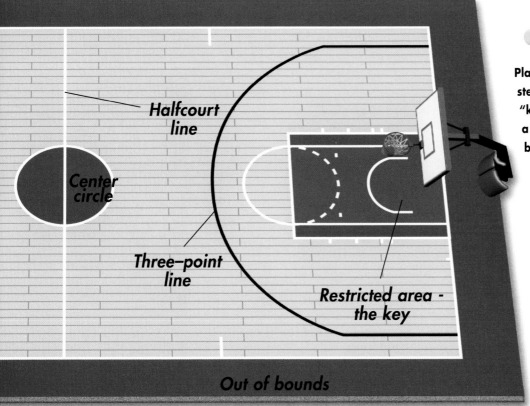

Halfcourt line

Center circle

Three-point line

Restricted area - the key

Out of bounds

**3 points**
*A basket scored from anywhere outside the three-point line.*

**2 points**
*A basket scored from anywhere inside the three-point line.*

**1 point**
*A basket scored from the free-throw line when a free throw is awarded after a foul.*

# EQUIPMENT

**B**asketball uniforms are often flashy and colorful, but they also need to fit well! Choose your uniform because it is comfortable, not because of how it looks.

## TRACKSUIT

Basketball players can spend a lot of time sitting on the bench, so it is important that they have tracksuits to keep their muscles warm when they are not playing. The tracksuit pants should be loose fitting, or at least have zippers or buttons along the side. This way, the pants can be removed quickly when a player is called to play.

## THE BALL

A full-sized basketball is made from leather, rubber, or a synthetic material. It is about 29–31 inches (75-78 cm) around and must be blown up to weigh between 20 and 22 oz (567–650 g).

## SHOES

The most important piece of equipment is the footwear. With so much running, jumping, twisting, and turning in basketball, make sure that you have the right kind of shoes. Shoes are usually made from a combination of leather and plastic. There are two main types of basketball shoes to choose from:

**LOW TOPS:**

Some players find lower–cut basketball shoes more comfortable. Make sure that these shoes still offer strong support around the ankle.

*Notice how strong the upper part of the shoe is. This design protects the feet from the quick action of a crowded basketball court.*

## JERSEY

A basketball jersey should be light and loose fitting. It is sleeveless so that the movement of the shoulders and arms is not restricted. The jersey should also feature tiny air holes to keep the body cool.

## PRACTICE HOOP

It is great for players to get a practice hoop set up at home or at school. The best kind can simply be fixed to a wall, with the hoop 10 feet (3.05 m) above the ground. The practice hoop should be set up where the ground is smooth (ideally concrete or tarmac) and away from any doors and windows.

## SHORTS

Shorts should be light, comfortable, and big enough to allow completely free movement.

## SOCKS

Socks are important in basketball because players' feet take such a pounding. They should be soft and thick to prevent blisters.

### HIGH-TOPS:

High-top basketball shoes give the ankles strong support, which basketball players need.

*The upper part of the shoe is tough and durable, but also soft, comfortable, and light.*

### SOLES:

Modern basketball shoes have air-cushioned soles to protect the ankles and soles of the feet when players land heavily after high jumps.

*The soles are made from rubber, offering a strong grip on the court surface.*

# DRIBBLING

**Y**ou are not allowed to walk or run while holding the ball in basketball—you must dribble the ball instead. Dribbling is one of the first skills that you need to master. It is important to keep the ball under control and away from opponents, and to be able to move quickly with your head up.

## BASIC DRIBBLING

You can only use one hand at a time while you are dribbling, and at least one foot must stay in contact with the court. Once you have stopped dribbling the ball, you must pass or shoot—you cannot start dribbling again.

**STEP 1**
*Do not look at the ball. Keep your head up so that you can see the other players on the court.*

**STEP 2**
*Using your fingers and your wrist, push the ball downward and slightly ahead of you with a clean, smooth motion.*

**STEP 3**
*Allow your fingers and wrist to move smoothly up and down with the ball. Do not let the ball make contact with the palm of your hand. Feel it with your fingers, and use your wrist to get pushing power.*

**STEP 4**
*As you move forward, bend your knees, and keep your body over the ball to shield it from opponents. Always dribble with the hand that is farthest from your opponent.*

**When there is an opponent in your way, you can beat him or her by stopping, changing hands, and dribbling away in the opposite direction.**

**STEP 1**

*As you dribble across your opponent, stop suddenly on the foot nearest him or her. Remember to keep the ball away from the other player.*

**STEP 2**

*Turn your body back the other way, pivoting (see page 12) on the foot nearest the player. Keep your back turned to him or her to shield the ball.*

**STEP 3**

*Keep turning until you are facing the opposite direction. As you bounce the ball at the end of your turn, collect it with your other hand and dribble away.*

## TOP TIP

**The reverse dribble should be done in one quick, smooth motion to fool and escape your opponent.**

# ON THE COURT: DRIBBLING

**T**hese simple drills are designed to help you practice dribbling and improve your ball control.

## DRIBBLING REACTION (2–6) PLAYERS

**This drill is great for helping you learn the most important rule of dribbling—look forward, not down at the ball.**

### STEP 1

*Players dribble the ball in a standing position and look forward at a coach or another player standing a few feet ahead.*

### STEP 2

*When the coach or other player raises his or her arm, the players stop dribbling. This way, the players must be watching closely to know when to stop.*

### PROGRESSION

*Instead just standing still, start walking or running toward the coach while dribbling.*

## DRIBBLING CONES (1–10) PLAYERS

**In a game situation, you will not be dribbling in a straight line very often!**

*Set up a line of cones, placing them about 2 feet (0.6 m) apart. Dribble in and out of them using one hand. Start off slowly, then speed up. As you improve, try switching hands. This technique makes dribbling through the cones easier.*

## DRIBBLING TAG (2–10) PLAYERS

**This drill teaches you to protect the ball while you dribble.**

*Mark out an area just big enough to contain the number of players. Each player has a ball, which her or she must dribble constantly. While dribbling and protecting his or her own ball, he or she must also try to knock the opponents' balls out of his or her hands. A player must leave the area when he or she either loses their ball or stops dribbling. The winner is the last player left dribbling a ball.*

## TRAFFIC JAM DRIBBLING (3–15) PLAYERS

This drill is good for all dribbling techniques, because it requires you to keep your head up, change hands and speeds, and protect the ball all at the same time.

### STEP 1

*Three or more players (each with a basketball) stand in a circle, ideally around the center circle. Players must dribble in a straight line to the other side of the circle, all starting at the same time.*

### STEP 2

*The players will all meet in the middle as they pass through the center of the circle.*

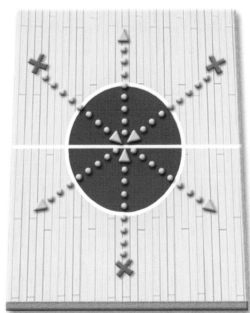

### STEP 3

*All players must dribble carefully to get through this "heavy traffic" and make it to the other side of the circle.*

### TOP TIP

**If you have enough players, make the circle two or three players deep. When the first players have made it through, they can pass the ball to the next set of players and go to the back of the line to wait for another turn.**

# BALL HANDLING

*Basketball is a fast—paced sport. As soon as you get the ball, you must get it under control and protect it from the opposition.*

## CATCHING GRIP

*This is the grip used by pro players. Place your non-shooting hand on the side of the ball, and grip it with your fingers. Place your shooting hand behind the ball, with your palm facing forward. This grip makes it easy to either pass or shoot quickly.*

shooting hand

## TRIPLE—THREAT POSITION

*The triple—threat position is the best body position to use when you receive the ball. Stand with your legs apart, and hold the ball firmly into your chest. Keep your body between the ball and your opponent. This position gives you time to decide your next move.*

## PIVOTING

When you stop with the ball, you are allowed to change direction without dribbling as long as you move only one foot. This is called "pivoting". You can use it to turn and "square up" to the basket.

**STEP 1**

*Once you have decided to turn, lift the heel of your pivot foot up and shift your body weight over it.*

**STEP 2**

*Lift your non-pivot foot up and begin to turn your body around, using short steps for balance.*

**STEP 3**

*Keep your knees bent, your back straight and your head up. Once you finsih the pivot, you should end up in the triple—threat position again.*

When you catch the ball in midair, you are allowed to take a step to stop. Using the stride stop allows you to stop legally, and it can also be used at the end of a dribble.

### STEP 1

*Move toward the pass. Stretch your hands out and keep your eyes on the incoming ball.*

### STEP 2

*As you catch it, step forward with your leading foot. This foot becomes your pivot foot and counts as a step.*

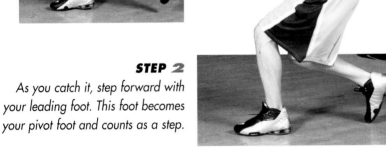

### STEP 3

*Bring yourself to a stop with your second step. You should end up in a balanced triple—threat position with your head up and your knees bent. Now you are ready to pass or shoot.*

The beauty of the jump stop is that it only counts as one step, so you can choose either foot as your pivot foot.

### STEP 1

*Jump toward the ball with both feet side by side.*

### STEP 2

*Catch the ball in midair, then make sure that you land with both feet touching the ground at the same time.*

### TOP TIP

*Once you have pivoted on one foot, you cannot switch and pivot on the other foot.*

# PASSING

*T*he easiest way for a basketball team to keep possession of the ball is by passing. Passes also move the ball up the court much quicker than dribbling does. There are three main types of pass—some passes are fast and direct, whereas others help you get the ball around opponents and to an open teammate.

## CHEST PASS

The chest pass is the safest and most accurate pass in basketball, but it can only be made when you have a clear path between yourself and the pass receiver.

### STEP 1

*Hold the ball to your chest with both hands. Your thumbs should be behind it, and your fingers should be on either side.*

### STEP 2

*Grip the ball firmly, and flex your wrists backward. Step forward and extend your arms sharply toward the receiver.*

### STEP 3

*As your arms straighten, release the ball firmly with a flick of the wrists. Your fingers should be pointing in the direction that you want the ball to go, with your thumbs downward.*

## TOP TIP

**Don't watch the ball as you make the pass— keep your eyes on your intended target.**

Sometimes you can't pass directly to a teammate because there is an opponent in the way. Use the overhead pass to get the ball over a player and to your teammate.

### STEP 1

*Hold the ball above your head with your fingers underneath it. Keep the ball out of reach of your opponent.*

### STEP 2

*Release the ball just above your head, using a sharp flick of the wrists and a short forward movement of the arms. Make sure that your eyes are on your target.*

Another way to pass when you are closely guarded is with the bounce pass.

### STEP 1

*When your opponent is stretching his or her arms out to stop a chest pass, bend your knees and extend your arm out to make the pass.*

### STEP 2

*Bounce the ball to your teammate. The ball will slow down when it hits the floor, so aim for the ball to hit the floor about two-thirds of the way to the receiver. This way, the pass will travel quickly past your opponent.*

# ON THE COURT: PASSING

*B*ecome a pass master with the help of these great passing exercises and drills.

## WALL PASSING (1 PERSON)

**STEP 1**
*Simply stand a few yards from the wall, and throw the ball against it. Imagine that you are passing through the wall to someone across from you.*

**STEP 2**
*As the ball bounces back off of the wall, catch it and repeat. Change your passes by using chest, overhead, and bounce passes.*

As you improve your passing and ball-handling skills, you will get used to catching powerful, difficult passes and passing the ball quickly.

## PIGGY IN THE MIDDLE (3 PLAYERS)

This is a classic drill and is great for sharpening up your passing skills. The player in the middle gets to work on defensive skills, too.

**STEP 1**
*Two players stand about 10 feet (3.5 m) apart. They must pass the ball to each other. A third player, the "piggy", stands between them and tries to block or intercept the pass.*

**STEP 2**
*When the player in the middle has touched the ball once, one of passing players becomes the new piggy.*

**TOP TIP**
**The passing players should not use overhead passes here because it is too easy to pass over the "piggy".**

This is a great drill for improving your passing and catching under pressure.

## TWO-PLAYER PASSING DRILL

### STEP 1
Two players stand about 10 feet (3.5 m) apart, both with basketballs in their hands. On the count of three, each player must pass the ball to the player opposite.

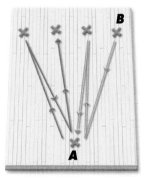

### STEP 2
One player must throw a chest pass while the other throws a bounce pass. As soon as the players catch the balls, they pass them back immediately. Keep this drill moving quickly and constantly.

Build up speed slowly to improve your reaction time.

## MACHINE-GUN PASSING (5 PLAYERS)

In a game of basketball, the action never stops. This lightning-quick passing drill helps you get used to thinking fast.

— Ball B    — Ball A

### STEP 1
Stand four players in a semi-circle, all facing a fifth player (player A) who stands about 8 feet (2.5 m) away. Both player A and one of the players in the semi-circle (player B) have a ball.

Each player should call the name of the intended receiver with each pass.

### STEP 2
After the whistle, player A passes the ball quickly to one of the players in the semi-circle, calling out the name of the intended receiver. As soon as that pass has been released, player B quickly passes his or her ball to player A. Player A receives it, then passes it to another player in the semi-circle. This cycle continues without resting. Players in the semi-circle can take turns being player A.

# SHOOTING

Anyone on a team can drain a basket. Perfecting your shooting techniques is important for scoring points.

## THE SET SHOT

**The set shot is used when you are standing still, relatively close to the basket. It is also the kind of shot that you would use for a free throw.**

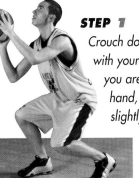

### STEP 1

*Crouch down facing the basket, with your knees slightly apart. If you are shooting with your right hand, your right leg should be slightly farther forward than your left leg.*

### STEP 2

*With your non-shooting hand gripping the side of the ball and your shooting hand facing toward the basket, begin to straighten your legs, and spring up toward the basket.*

### STEP 3

*Lift yourself up onto your toes in one movement. Use your non-shooting hand to steady the ball, then shoot with a strong flick of the wrist.*

## THE JUMP SHOT

**Often the only way to get your shot past an opponent in front of you is to jump and release the ball in midair.**

### STEP 1

*Face the basket with your feet flat on the floor. Crouch down low to give yourself enough force to jump off the court.*

### STEP 2

*Straighten up, and bring the ball into the shooting position. Have the elbow of your shooting arm directly beneath the ball.*

### STEP 3

*Spring off the ground to shoot above the reach of any defender. Focus on the basket as you release the ball.*

Unlike the previous two shots, the layup is used when you are on the move. This shot is all about driving right to the basket and using the backboard to help you score.

### STEP 1

*Approach the basket from the side as you dribble toward it. Put all of your weight on your front leg—if you are right-handed then this should be your left leg—and bend your knee to give you the spring to jump.*

### STEP 2

*Spring off of your front leg and raise your arms, ready to throw the ball.*

**Your layup should be one continuous and smooth movement. Keep your eyes on the basket at all times.**

### STEP 3

*Jump up toward the side of the basket, not directly in front of the hoop. As you reach the top of your jump, move the ball to your shooting hand. Extend your arm as far as it will go, and release the ball.*

### STEP 4

*The ball should bounce off of the backboard and go softly into the hoop.*

### TOP TIP

**Aim for the small rectangle on the backboard. The perfect layup should hit the top corner of the rectangle nearest you.**

# ON THE COURT: SHOOTING

**Y**ou want to make all of your shots in a basketball game count. After you miss a shot, your team can quickly lose the ball. That is why even the world's top pro players practice shooting regularly to perfect their skills.

## ONE-PLAYER DRILL

**Stand close to the basket, and practice set shots and jump shots from the same point.**

*Keep shooting until you can get five of each in a row, then move to another spot. Move farther out from the basket or change your angle. Try shooting with your non-shooting hand as well. This will be difficult at first, but it improves your skills.*

Every time you shoot, picture the ball going into the basket. If you believe that you are going to score, you probably will.

## AROUND THE WORLD (1-2 PLAYERS

**This drill teaches you to vary your shooting distance and angle around the basket.**

*Stand on one of the marks on the key closest to the basket, and shoot. If you score, fetch the ball and move on to the next mark. If you miss, remain on your spot until the next go. See how quickly you can score baskets going around the key from spots 1 to 10. Once you set a record, try to beat it!*

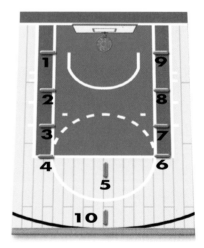

### TOP TIP
*Try racing a friend "around the world". This added pressure teaches you to get into position and shoot quickly, just like you would in a real game.*

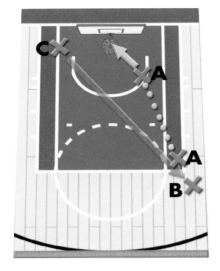

**Keep things moving with this layup drill, which also provides rebounding and passing practice.**

*Two players (A and B) stand on the edge of the key to the right of the basket, while a third (player C) stands just to the left of the basket. Player A approaches the basket and attempts a layup shot. Player C collects the ball and passes it back to player B. Player B now runs at the basket, while player A moves under the basket to replace player C. Player C moves to the edge of the key to receive and immediately play the ball. The cycle continues so that everyone gets to practice layups.*

**This is another fast-moving drill involving three players—two providers and one shooter—and two balls. This drill allows the shooter to get into a good rhythm.**

**Try to increase the speed of passing and shooting to build up the rhythm.**

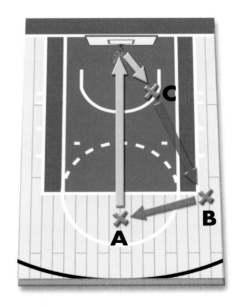

*The shooter (player A) stands on the edge of the key. Player B stands on the other side of the key, and player C waits under the basket. Player A shoots, player C collects the ball and passes it quickly to player B. Player B passes it swiftly on to player A who shoots again. When player A has five attempts, all players move around one position, and the drill starts again.*

# REBOUNDING

**W**hen someone takes a shot, there's a good chance that it will bounce off of the backboard or the hoop. This is called a "rebound". Grabbing rebounds is an important skill, because it helps your team get the ball.

## BOXING OUT

When a player shoots, you must attempt to put yourself between the basket and your opponent. This skill is called "boxing out", and it is used to win the rebound.

### STEP 1

*As the shot is made, anticipate a rebound by positioning your body between the hoop and your opponent.*

### STEP 2

*Bend your knees and spread your arms, making your body big and strong. Watch the ball at all times, and get ready to jump up as the ball rebounds.*

## DEFENSIVE REBOUNDING

When you catch a rebound from an opponent's shot, you regain possession for your team. This defensive play can instantly turn into an attack.

### STEP 1

*By boxing out your opponent, you have made yourself the favorite to win the ball if it rebounds. When it does, aim to catch it at the highest point possible. Doing this is all about timing your jump. Don't jump too early, or you may find yourself on the way down as the ball reaches catching height.*

### STEP 2

*As you catch the ball, turn away from your nearest opponent so that the ball is protected as you land.*

It is also important for attacking players to follow up on rebounds. Keeping control of the ball means that the attack stays alive, and your team can still score.

*Just like defensive rebounding, the secrets to successful offensive–rebound play are position, anticipation, and timing. Escape the defender who is trying to block you by moving slightly one way, then darting quickly in the other direction. Try to box out so that you are better placed to time your jump and win the ball. If you win the ball and have enough space, you can jump straight back up and shoot!*

## TIPPING IN

If you are on the attack near the hoop and you judge the rebound perfectly, you can try a tip in. Instead of catching the ball, landing, and then shooting, you can just try to tip the ball straight back into the basket. Be warned, this skill is tough!

*Tipping in is a difficult skill to perfect. It requires good judgement and a spectacular jump. Watch the flight of the shot, and launch yourself into the air just as the ball hits the rim or the backboard. Adjust your body in midair and try to get a hand to the ball. If you can get there, guide the ball back into the basket with a gentle flick of the hand.*

### TOP TIP
**The secret of tipping in is to guide the ball into the basket, not shoot it in. You often only need the lightest touch to guide the bouncing ball back into the basket.**

# ON THE COURT: REBOUNDING

I t may be more fun to practice shooting and dribbling, but rebounding is just as critical to great basketball. Be sure to spend time sharpening up your rebounding with these drills.

### ONE-PLAYER DRILL

When your have perfected your rebounding, practice shooting as soon as you have landed, or pivoting back toward the opposite end of the court as if you were defending.

**STEP 2**

As the ball rebounds, jump and catch it. Work on timing your leap so that you jump forward to meet the ball and catch it at the highest point you can.

**STEP 1**

Stand under the basket, 5 feet (1.5 m) away from the baseline, and shoot the ball against the backboard.

### TIPPING-IN DRILL (2-10 PLAYERS)

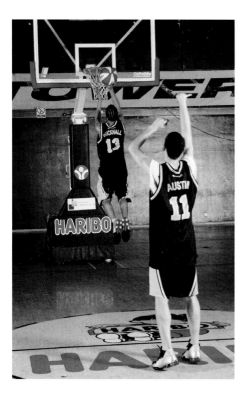

A line of players, each with a ball, stands next to the free-throw line. One by one, they pass their balls to a player standing on the free-throw line. This player shoots at the backboard so that the ball rebounds. The player who has passed the ball follows up on the shot, jumps, and tries to tip in the

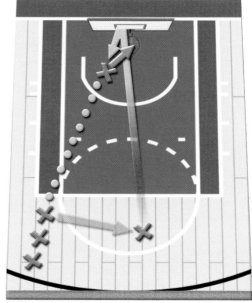

ball. Then the player collects the ball and goes to the back of the line while the next player continues the routine. If the rebound cannot be tipped in, players should catch the ball and shoot.

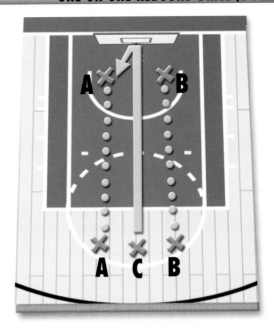

Two opposing players (A and B) stand in the center of the key, 6 feet (1.8 m) away from the basket. While they try to box each other out, a third player (C) shoots at the backboard from the free-throw line. Players A and B must compete to catch the rebound. After a while, try these variations to the drill:

### VARIATION 1

Change the drill by making A an attacking player and B defensive. While A must try to tip in or shoot from the rebound, B must try to catch the ball or block A's attempts at scoring.

### VARIATION 2

Add two more players, one attacking and one defending, to recreate a game rebound situation.

# DEFENDING

**E**very basketball player must be able to defend when the other team has the ball. Defensive skills are just as important to winning games as shooting and rebounding are.

## DEFENSIVE STANCE

This body position that makes it difficult for an opponent to pass or shoot around you. Bend your knees and stay on your toes so that you can react quickly. Stand with one arm raised and one arm lowered and with both hands open. Now your arms are able to prevent both a chest and a bounce pass.

## PREVENTING A PASS RECEPTION

If you are guarding a player who is ready to receive the ball, position yourself alongside your opponent so that you can get your arm across to prevent the pass. Stay on your toes, and keep close to your opponent without commiting a foul.

## DEFENCE AGAINST A DRIBBLER

**STEP 1**

Get your body between the ball and the basket, and take up the defensive stance. Move with your opponent as he or she dribbles. Don't get too close, because it will be easier for your opponent to get around you. Just try to block your opponent's path to the basket.

**STEP 2**

Bend your knees, and keep your feet flat on the floor. By shuffling instead of taking big steps, you can quickly react to your opponent's changes of speed and direction.

When your opponent has the ball, you should make it as hard as possible for him or her to pass it to a teammate.

> Watch your opponent's chest, not the ball. That way you are less likely to fall for a fake or dummy shot.

**STEP 1**

*Adopt the defensive stance, and keep on your toes so that you can react to your opponent's moves and fakes.*

**STEP 2**

*Use your arms and hands to block any attempt at passing or shooting.*

*Be aggressive and physical without actually touching your opponent. If you do, a foul will be awarded against you. The secret of great defending is to use your brain as well as your body. If you can anticipate your opponent's next move, you will know how to stop it.*

## TOP TIP
**When defending, keep an eye on both the passer and the pass receiver as much as possible.**

# ON THE COURT: DEFENDING

*I*t is necessary that basketball players work on their defensive games. Here are some
drills that make it fun to defend.

## ZIG-ZAG (2 PLAYERS)

This is a great drill for both defending and dribbling. Mark out an
area about 12 feet (3.5 m) wide and about half the court long. An
offensive player must dribble the entire length of this area, traveling
in a zig-zag pattern. At the same time, a defensive player guards
this player and attempts to stop the dribble or steal the ball.

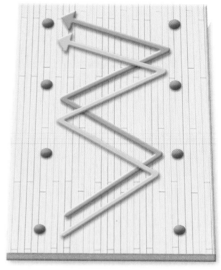

—— **Offensive player**
—— **Defensive player**

## DENIAL DRILL (3 PLAYERS)

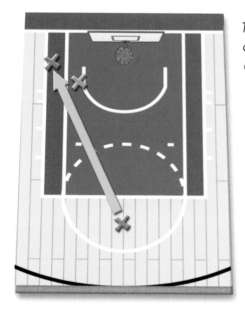

*This drill requires two
offensive players and a
defensive player. The
defender must try to stop a
pass reception. One
offensive player with the
ball stands about 16 feet
(5 m) from the other. The
defensive player must get
in front of the pass
receiver. The defender
moves constantly to make
it difficult for the pass to
get through.*

**TOP TIP**
*If you are defending, try to be roughly two steps in front of your opponent—facing
the passer—and only one step away from the line of the intended pass.*

Playing two-on-two basketball is a great way to develop all of the skills required in the game of basketball—from dribbling and shooting, to passing and rebounding. It is an excellent drill for improving your defending, because you are under serious pressure when your team does not have the ball.

## STEP 1

Two teams of two players play a mini game of basketball in which both teams shoot on the same basket. All players stay within the area of the key. The game is started from the free-throw line and, if one team scores or puts the ball out of play, the other team restarts play.

**Work together as a team. When you are defending, guard the nearest player and then stick with that opponent until you get a chance to intercept the ball.**

## STEP 2

When the other team has the ball, stay focused on good defensive skills with your teammate. If either of you lose your concentration or your position for a second, your opponents will score easily.

# ADVANCED DRIBBLING

*N*ow that you have mastered the basics, it's time to really go to school! You should now feel comfortable enough handling the basketball to try some pro techniques.

## ADVANCED DRIBBLING

When you run in a straight line and dribble the ball with the same hand, it is very easy for a defender to block your path or steal the ball. If you switch dribbling hands, and bounce the ball between your legs or behind your back, your opposition will have a much tougher time stopping you.

## CROSSOVER DRIBBLING

### STEP 1
*As you dribble forward, keep your legs apart and your body low. Bring the ball to your side.*

### STEP 2
*Still moving forward, bounce the ball across the front of your body and into your other hand.*

### STEP 3
*Immediately bounce the ball back to the other hand, and continue moving forward.*

### STEP 1

As you dribble, step forward, bringing the ball to your side.

### STEP 2

Bounce the ball sideways between the gap in your legs. Bring your receiving hand down to collect it.

### STEP 3

Allow the ball to bounce out to your side, giving you room to take another step forward.

**This is a tricky skill to perfect, so start off slowly. The temptation is to look down at the ball, but make sure that you don't!**

### STEP 4

Bounce the ball through your legs again and back to your other hand. Make the gap between your legs as wide as you can, and guide the ball cleanly through it.

### STEP 1

With your legs wide apart and your body position low, bring the ball out to your side.

### STEP 2

Looking straight ahead, bounce the ball gently behind you. Bring your other hand behind your back to receive it.

### STEP 3

As the ball touches your receiving hand, bring your arm up with the bounce and out to the side of your body.

### STEP 4

Using the palm of your hand on the top of the ball, dribble it back the other way as in steps 2 and 3.

# FAKE & DRIVE

The basic skills of basketball allow you to play the game, but if you master these advanced skills, you can become a real clutch player for your team. The fake and drive is a useful skill to master for offensive play.

**FAKE & DRIVE**

The fake and drive is a tactic that is used to confuse your opponent and give yourself space to drive for the basket.

### STEP 1

*When your path is blocked by a defender, you must quickly find a clear route to the basket.*

### STEP 2

*Take a fake step to one side, as though you are about to start dribbling forward. The defender will move to block you.*

**TOP TIP**
Make sure that you don't push your opponent aside as you drive forward. This will give you a foul and your opposition the ball!

### STEP 3

As your opponent moves, stop and quickly move back the other way, keeping the ball in the hand farthest away. This move will catch your opponent by surprise.

### STEP 4

Take a big first step to dribble past your opponent and drive toward the basket. Your opponent will still be caught off guard.

### STEP 5

A successful fake gives you the vital split second to escape your defender/opponent. Now drive straight for the basket. Keep your head up and look for a chance to shoot or pass.

# TIP OFF

A basketball game is started and restarted after each quarter with a jump ball. Win the jump ball, and you can put your team in the driver's seat for quick points.

## JUMP BALL

*The referee throws the ball up between two players in the center circle. They must jump up and try to tip it to their teammates. The two players must not touch the ball until it reaches its highest point, and can only touch it twice. After that, it can only be touched by another player.*

### STEP 1
Crouch opposite your opponent. Have your body weight over your toes so that you can easily spring up to the ball when it comes into play.

### STEP 2
As the ball is tossed into the air, time your jump so that you meet the ball at its highest point. Watch the ball as you jump. Extend your body and your arms so that you are at full stretch when it starts to come down. If you reach the ball first, tip it to your teammates who are waiting around the edge of the center circle.

Be careful not to jump too soon. Otherwise you will be falling back down when you should be at the top of your jump, and you will miss the ball!

# ADVANCED SHOOTING

I*f you pull off a hook shot or a slam dunk, you'll do more then score two points—*
*you'll be king of the court!*

**THE HOOK SHOT**

**When the direct route to the hoop is blocked, the hook shot is an excellent way to still take a shot on the basket.**

### STEP 1

*Move away from your opponent by pivoting. Keep your back turned to your opponent to protect the ball.*

### STEP 2

*As you turn, transfer the ball to your shooting hand and cup it with your outstretched fingers. Extend your arm straight out behind you as you lift your back leg off the ground.*

### STEP 3

*As you spring off your forward leg, keep your arm straight and the ball cupped in your shooting hand. Toss the ball over your head toward the hoop. Release the ball at full stretch and at the top of your jump.*

**THE SLAM DUNK**

**The slam dunk is the most famous shot in basketball because it is the most spectacular. However, you must either be very tall or a superb jumper to pull it off.**

### STEP 1

*Approach the basket running as fast as you can, springing off on your left leg if you have the ball in your right hand and vice versa.*

### STEP 2

*You need to jump high enough to get the whole ball over the height of the hoop.*

### STEP 3

*If you have gone high enough, you will literally be able to slam the ball down into the basket. Slam dunk!*

# FAST BREAK DRILLS

Often, the best way to score points is to gain possession during an opposition attack and move quickly down the court while the other team are trying to get back in position. This is called a "fast break". These two drills are designed to improve your ability to perform great fast breaks.

## TWO-ON-ONE DRILL (3 PLAYERS)

### STEP 1

*Two offensive players (A and B) stand on the baseline, one on each corner of the key. A defensive player (C) stands on the other baseline under the basket. On the whistle, A and B move the ball up toward player C as fast as they can, passing the ball between them as they go.*

### STEP 2

*When players A and B reach the halfcourt line, player C moves forward to the top of the key to defend against them.*

### STEP 3

*Players A and B attack the basket as they would in a game. They must pass, dribble and shoot their way to a basket as quickly as possible. As soon as they have scored or player C has won the ball, repeat the drill.*

**FAST–BREAK DRILL (5 PLAYERS)**

### STEP 1

Three offensive players line up on the baseline, while two defensive players line up on the edge of the key at the opposite end of the court.

### STEP 2

On the coach's instruction, the three offensive players move the ball upcourt as quickly as they can, creating a three-on-two situation around the opposite basket.

### STEP 3

The attacking players must work together to score a basket.

### STEP 4

As soon as a basket is scored, the scoring offensive player joins the previously defensive pair to create a three-on-two attacking situation at the other end.

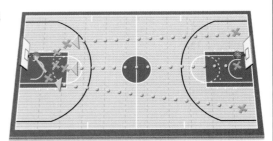

### STEP 5

The two remaining offensive players now become the two defenders and must get back to defend the basket at the other end.

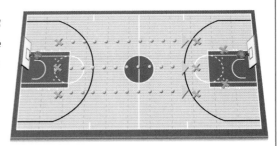

## TOP TIP

Speed is the key to both of these drills. Even though it's only a practice, play with the same energy as you would in a real game.

# FOULS

Basketball is a non-contact sport, but with ten players moving quickly in such a tight area, some body contact will occur. However, when players unfairly get in the way of their opponents—either intentionally or unintentionally—a personal foul is called.

## PERSONAL FOULS

### BLOCKING

*Any kind of contact that slows the progress of an attacking opponent.*

### CHARGING

*When a player, with or without the ball, pushes or moves into a defending opponent.*

### HAND CHECKING

*The use of the hands by a defending player on an opponent, either to impede his or her progress or assist in his or her guarding of that opponent.*

### GUARDING FROM THE REAR

*Contact from the rear by a defensive player. The guarding player is always held responsible for such contact.*

### HOLDING
Personal contact with an opponent—on any part of his or her body—that interferes with his or her freedom of movement.

### ILLEGAL SCREENING
Any attempt to illegally delay or prevent an opponent who does not have control of the ball from reaching his or her desired position on the court.

### PUSHING
Contact when a player forcibly moves or attempts to move an opponent, whether or not he or she has control of the ball.

### ILLEGAL USE OF HANDS
When a player makes contact with an opponent with his or her hand(s) while attempting to play the ball.

## DOUBLE FOULS

A double foul is a situation in which two opposing players commit fouls against each other at the same time. When this happens, a personal foul is called against each of the players, but no free throws are awarded. Instead, play is restarted by a jump ball at the nearest circle to the two players involved.

# WARMING UP & STRETCHING

*Warming up and stretching before a practice session or a game is very important. It reduces the risk of injury and increases a player's speed and ability to twist and turn.*

## WARMING UP

Before you pick up a ball or even begin stretching, it is important to warm up your body. This dramatically lessens your chance of pulling a muscle or a tendon. All you need to do is a light jog around the court for five minutes. This will increase your heart rate and get the blood pumping around your body.

## STRETCHING

**You must be very careful with your stretching.**

– *Never stretch until the body is warmed up.*

– *Always stretch slowly and gently and never so much that it is uncomfortable.*

– *Hold each stretch for 10 to 20 seconds, keeping your body steady at all times.*

– *Never rock or bounce on a stretch.*

– *Breathe out as you stretch.*

– *Stretch both before and after exercise.*

**There are hundred of stretches that you can do, but here are some of the most important. Ask a coach or a physiotherapist to show you others and to check that you are doing these properly!**

## GROIN STRETCH

Stand with your legs apart. Then, placing one hand on your thigh, dip your shoulder and lean to one side until you feel slight tension in your groin muscles on that side. Hold the stretch there, then repeat on the other side.

## HAMSTRING STRETCH

*Lie on your back, and gently lift one leg up in the air. Use your hands to keep the leg straight until you feel tension in your hamstring at the back of your leg. Hold the stretch there, then repeat with the other leg.*

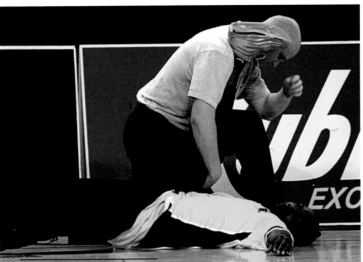

## TWO'S COMPANY

*Some stretches can be done with a teammate or coach to keep the stretch steady and straight.*

## TOUCH YOUR TOES

*Gently bend down as if you were going to touch your toes, but stop when you feel tension in the backs of your legs. Hold the stretch for 10 seconds and then try reaching down a little more. Gradually, you should be able to reach down farther and farther until you can actually get right down.*

## CALF STRETCH

*Put the weight of your body on the front foot, bending the knee and stretching the other leg behind with your heel up. Then lean forward so that your hands touch the ground and slowly push your outstretched leg back.*

## PRACTICE SHOTS

*Warming up your body before a match is most important. But it is also important to practice shooting hoops. This gets your brain into gear and your hand-eye coordination up to speed.*

# DIET & MENTAL ATTITUDE

Eating certain foods won't make you a skilled player, but you can give yourself more energy and stamina on the court by eating and drinking the right foods. This food chart gives you the basic principles of a balanced diet that is ideal for athletes.

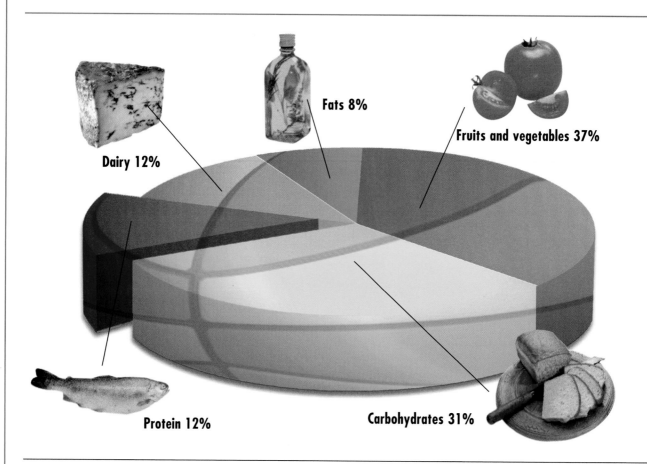

Dairy 12%

Fats 8%

Fruits and vegetables 37%

Protein 12%

Carbohydrates 31%

## ENERGY BUSTERS

**If you are doing a lot of exercise, then you need to cut down on fatty foods and eat plenty of carbohydrates to provide the energy for all of the exercise that you are doing.**

*Although you do need protein for the growth and repair of the body after exercise, try to choose low-fat sources, such as fish or chicken.*

## BEFORE THE GAME

**Basketball is a non-stop, end-to-end game, which means that you need to eat a high-carbohydrate meal at least three hours before playing to provide enough energy to see you through the game.**

*Low-fat pasta or rice dishes (without creamy sauce) are ideal. Just before the game, boost your carbohydrate level with quick-digesting snacks such as bananas or dried fruit. It is also important to drink plenty of liquid before and during a game. Drink water or isotonic sports drinks two or three hours before playing to make up for the water that you will sweat away during the game.*

## MENTAL ATTITUDE

**As well as preparing the body, it is also important to prepare the mind for a basketball game.**

*In all sports, much of your ability as a player comes from self-confidence and belief. If you believe that you are going to win the match or that you are going to sink that free throw, chances are that you will.*

## MENTAL PREPARATION

**More and more sports coaches are using methods of coaching that focus on the psychological side as well as the physical. Pro basketball clubs will often use a sports psychologist to work with the players on their positive thinking and concentration, as well as building up faith in themselves and their teammates.**

*Basketball is such a quick game that it is essential not to lose concentration for a moment. Try to focus all the time, never letting your mind drift from the game for even a second. Some teams also like to focus together, gathering into a huddle before the match or at the end of a time out. Basketball is a team game, and it is important that the team works together. If your team believes in one another, you will be more prepared to play your hardest for your teammates, and they will be prepared to do the same for you.*

# HOW THE PROS DO IT

**M**ost people just play basketball for fun, but imagine if you got to play every day and got paid for it! It's a great life for players in the NBA, but don't think that it is all glamor and glory in the pro game. It takes hard work and dedication to make it and stay at the top of the sport.

**The peak of world basketball is the NBA. It features the best teams and arenas in the world, as well as the best players.** *But it is not all bright lights and slam dunking for these stars. An NBA player has to work hard. Each team plays 82 games every season—even more if they reach the playoffs. Away games are played all over the U.S. and in Canada—that means lots of time on the road. To play this often at such a high level, players must be incredibly fit—like the high-scoring Boston Celtics player, Kevin Garnett. Even during the off season, players are expected to work on their fitness. Many pros spend their summers training and working hard on the skills that they still wish to improve.*

## TYPICAL NBA GAME DAY (HOME)

**9:00**    Wake up.

**9:30**    Eat breakfast.

**10:00** Drive to practice.

**11:00** Team practice, including stretching, jogging, shooting, and rebounding. Work on new plays, some sprints, and finish with free throws.

**12:00** Watch videos of recent games of tonight's opponents.

**1:00**    Drive back home to rest.

**2:00**    Eat a high-carbohydrate lunch and drink plenty of liquids.

**5:00**    Return to the arena and get changed.

**6:00**    Go out on the court to warm up and take practice shots.

**7:00**    Head back into the locker room where the coach will go over last-minute tactics.

**7:40**    Showtime! The introduction to an NBA game is like a star-studded Hollywood movie premiere. The lights dim, music blares, and a multimedia laser-light show leads to the introduction of the starting five players from each team.

**8:00**    Four quarters of NBA action.

**11:00** Media interviews. Win or lose, players are required to speak to the media after the game.

**12:00** Shower and eat a team meal.

**12:30** Go home, or board a team bus. Tomorrow could bring another game in another city.

## MEDIA WORK

**If you are a top basketball player in the NBA, everyone wants to know your opinion of the game.**

There are hundreds of TV and radio shows, newspapers, magazines, and Internet websites dedicated to basketball. Part of a player's job is to answer questions and pose for photographs. TV companies pay large amounts to show pro basketball games. As part of the deal, cameras will often be allowed access to the courtside and dressing-room areas, where players and coaches give interviews.

## MONEY

**Top basketball players, such as Shaquille O'Neal of the Miami Heat (*right*), earn millions of dollars every season. In addition to their basketball earnings, they also endorse products like sportswear or shoes.**

*However, basketball athletes playing in less high-profile leagues in Europe and around the world are not so wealthy.*

# RULES

There are hundreds of rules in basketball, and we don't have room for them all here. These are the basics, and they are always enforced by the referees.

## TIMING

An NBA basketball game is divided into four quarters of 12 minutes each (international matches have four quarters of 10 minutes each). However, the clock is stopped often during a game, and in real time, most games last about 90 minutes. If the scores are tied at the end of regulation time, the teams play five–minute overtime periods until there is a winner. There are no ties in basketball.

## TIMEOUTS

Timeouts are moments when a coach can stop play to discuss tactics with the team. In the NBA, teams are given six 60–second timeouts in a game, plus one 20–second timeout per half. In overtime, they get three more 60–second timeouts per period.

## FREE THROW

A free throw is an unchallenged shot at the basket, taken from behind the free-throw line on the edge of the key. All players, other than the shooter, must stand outside the key in the designated free-throw lanes, or outside the three point line. Free throws are awarded for various fouls, and a basket scores one point.

## 24-SECOND RULE

In the NBA, when a team gains possession of the ball, they have 24 seconds to shoot the ball at the basket. If they fail to do so, they lose possession.

## EIGHT-SECOND RULE

After gaining possession inside their own half of the court, the attacking team must move the ball into the opposition's half within eight seconds. Again, if they fail to do so, they lose possession.

## FIVE-SECOND RULE

A player must take a throw-in or a free throw within five seconds. In the NBA, players have 10 seconds to take a free throw.

## THREE-SECOND RULE

Players are allowed to be in their opposition's restricted area—the key—for only three seconds at a time. If they stay longer, their team loses possession.

## CLOSELY-GUARDED PLAYER

In international basketball, if a player is closely guarded, he must either pass, dribble or shoot within five seconds of receiving the ball, or possession is given to the opposition. This rule does not exist in the NBA.

## PERSONAL FOUL

This is an infringement of the rules involving body contact with an opponent (see pages 38–39). Such fouls are punished with either a throw-in to the opposition, or if the fouled player was in the process of shooting, one or more free throws to be taken by the fouled player. For example, three free throws if the shot was being attempted from outside the three point line.

## TECHNICAL FOUL

This is an infringement of the rules involving bad behavior, such as arguing with opponents or officials. These fouls are punished with two free throws taken by a player chosen by the opposing team's captain.

## DISQUALIFYING FOUL

This is a serious foul on an opponent, such as a punch, punished by instant dismissal from the game.

## SIX-FOUL RULE

When a player has committed six fouls (either personal or technical), he or she is dismissed from the game and may not return. In international basketball, the rule is five fouls.

## VIOLATION

A foul awarded for a violation of the rules, such as an illegal dribble or spending more than three seconds in the restricted area. A violation is punished by awarding the ball to the opposition, usually with a throw-in.

## GOALTENDING

Players must not touch the ball when it is on its downward flight toward the basket. Defenders also are not allowed to touch the ball when it is in the basket—otherwise they would be able to push the ball back out through the hoop! This violation is called "goaltending". If goaltending is committed by the offensive team, no points are scored, and the ball is awarded to the opposition at the free-throw line. If it is committed by the defence, the shooter is awarded the same points as if the ball had gone through the basket.

## OUT OF BOUNDS

A player is out of bounds if he or she touches or crosses any boundary line, taking the ball off of the court. The ball is out of bounds when the player in possession goes out of bounds, or the ball itself touches or crosses a boundary line. However, the ball cannot be out of bounds until it touches the floor. When this happens, the throw-in is given to the team who did not touch the ball last.

## OVER AND BACK

When a team has moved the ball from inside their own half of the court into their opposition's half, they are not allowed to move back over the halfcourt line. If they do, the ball goes to the other team.

# GLOSSARY

**ASSIST** – A pass that leads to a teammate scoring.

**BASKET** – The hoop and net through which the ball must go to score points. Also the name for scoring.

**BACKBOARD** – The rectangle behind the basket off of which the ball is allowed to rebound.

**BACK COURT** – The half of the court that a team defends.

**BOXING OUT** – The positioning of a player between the basket and an opponent to win a rebound.

**BOUNCE PASS** – A pass where the ball is bounced off of the ground to a teammate.

**CHEST PASS** – A short, direct pass made at chest height.

**COURT** – The playing area for a basketball game.

**DEFENCE** – When a team has the ball, the other team is on defence to try to stop them from scoring.

**DRIBBLING** – Moving around the court while dribbling the ball.

**DRIVE** – An aggressive dribble directly toward the basket.

**FAKE** – When a player pretends to move or throw the ball one way, but stops an goes the other way to fool an opponent.

**FIELD GOAL** – Any basket scored, with the exception of free throws, from anywhere on the court

**FOUL** – An illegal play.

**FREE THROW** – An unopposed shot taken from behind the free-throw line. Given after an opposing foul.

**FRONT COURT** – The half of the court that a team is attacking.

**HOOK SHOT** – A shot where the ball is played over a players' head facing the basket sideways.

**HOOP** – The circular section of the basket that the ball must go through to score.

**JUMP BALL** – Used to start and restart the game, with two opposing players jumping against each other to win a ball thrown by the referee.

**JUMP SHOT** – A shot played while the shooter is jumping in the air.

**KEY** – The painted restricted area underneath the basket at each end.

**LAYUP** – When you take one and a half steps toward the net and shoot the ball off of the backboard into the basket.

**NBA** – National Basketball Association.

**OFFENCE** – When a team is in possession of the ball, they are on offence and trying to score.

**OVERHEAD PASS** – A pass to a teammate played above the head.

**OVERTIME** – An extra period of five minutes that is played if the scores are tied after regulation time.

**PIVOTING** – Turning on the spot while holding the ball.

**REBOUND** – A shot that misses the basket and bounces back off of the hoop or backboard.

**REFEREE** – The official in charge of a basketball game. At the pro level, there may be more than one referee in a game.

**SET SHOT** – A straight shot at the basket, taken with both feet on the ground.

**SLAM DUNK** – A shot where the ball is held above the basket and then forced downward through it.

**STEAL** – Legally gaining possession of the ball from a dribbler or passer.

**THREE POINTER** – See 'Field goal'.

**THROW-IN** – A throw from the sideline to re-start play.

**TIMEOUT** – A break in play called by the coach.

**TIP IN** – A shot where the ball is rebounded off of the backboard into the basket.

**TRIPLE–THREAT POSITION** – The standard position to protect the ball, taken when players receive the ball.

# INDEX

Printed in the USA